NOV 2 8 2016

Spotlight on the
MAYA, AZTEC, and INCA CIVILIZATIONS

Ancient AZTEC CULTURE

Emily Mahoney

PowerKiDS press™

NEW YORK

Published in 2017 by The Rosen Publishing Group, Inc.
29 East 21st Street, New York, NY 10010

Editor: Katie Kawa
Book Design: Tanya Dellaccio

Photo Credits: Cover Dan Kitwood/Staff/Getty Images; p. 5 https://commons.wikimedia.org/wiki/File:Murales_Rivera_-_Markt_in_Tlatelolco_3.jpg; p. 6 pavalena/Shutterstock.com; p. 7 (top) https://commons.wikimedia.org/wiki/File:Rekonstruktion_Tempelbezirk_von_Tenochtitlan_2_Templo_Mayor_3.jpg; p. 7 (bottom) gary yim/Shutterstock.com; p. 8 https://commons.wikimedia.org/wiki/File:Codex_Mendoza_folio_67r_bottom.jpg; pp. 9, 18, 25 DEA/G. DAGLI ORTI/Getty Images; p. 10 Gary Friedman/Getty Images; p. 11 (top) https://commons.wikimedia.org/wiki/File:Codex_Magliabechiano_folio_13r.jpg; p. 11 (bottom) https://commons.wikimedia.org/wiki/File:Codex_Magliabechiano_folio_12r.jpg; p. 13 ullstein bild/Getty Images; p. 14 courtesy of the Library of Congress; p. 15 (both) Julio Aldana/Shutterstock.com; p. 16 https://commons.wikimedia.org/wiki/File:Aztec_-_Mask_-_Walters_2009201.jpg; p. 17 https://commons.wikimedia.org/wiki/File:Codex_Borgia_page_52.jpg; p. 21 Grafissimo/Getty Images; p. 22 https://commons.wikimedia.org/wiki/File:Double_headed_turquoise_serpentAztecbritish_museum.jpg; p. 23 https://commons.wikimedia.org/wiki/File:20041229-Coatlicue_(Museo_Nacional_de_Antropolog%C3%ADa)_MQ-3.jpg; p. 24 https://commons.wikimedia.org/wiki/File:Florentine_Codex_IX_Aztec_Warriors.jpg; p. 26 Dorling Kindersley/Getty Images; p. 27 https://commons.wikimedia.org/wiki/File:Macuilxochitl_Patolli.png; p. 29 Print Collector/Getty Images.

Library of Congress Cataloging-in-Publication Data

Names: Mahoney, Emily Jankowski, author.
Title: Ancient Aztec culture / Emily Mahoney.
Description: New York : PowerKids Press, 2016. | Series: Spotlight on the
  Maya, Aztec, and Inca civilizations | Includes index.
Identifiers: LCCN 2016002135 | ISBN 9781499418958 (pbk.) | ISBN 9781499418989 (library bound) | ISBN 9781499418965 (6 pack)
Subjects: LCSH: Aztecs--Juvenile literature. | Aztecs--Social life and
  customs--Juvenile literature.
Classification: LCC F1219.73 .M3364 2016 | DDC 972/.01--dc23
LC record available at http://lccn.loc.gov/2016002135

CPSIA Compliance Information: Batch #BS16PK For further information contact Rosen Publishing, New York, New York at 1-800-237-9932.

CONTENTS

THE AZTEC CIVILIZATION

The Aztec Empire ruled part of **Mesoamerica**—specifically what's now central and southern Mexico—from around the 13th century to the 16th century. The Aztecs were overthrown by Spanish **conquistadors** in 1521, but during their rule, they made important discoveries, developed religious **customs**, and created a **unique** culture, or way of life. Despite the fact that the Aztec people lived many centuries ago, their society and culture were very advanced. Many people wonder how they were able to accomplish so much in their relatively short time of prosperity.

The Aztec civilization was made up of a collection of city-states, or independent states consisting of a city and surrounding areas. These city-states were connected to form the Aztec Empire, but historians believe these people didn't call themselves "Aztecs." Instead, the people we consider the Aztecs are believed to have called themselves the Mexica people.

> Historians believe that—at its peak—the Aztec Empire stretched for over 80,000 square miles (207,199 sq km).

CREATING A CAPITAL

The Aztecs settled near Lake Texcoco and began building what would become their capital city, Tenochtitlán, in 1325. The most impressive sight in the city was Templo Mayor, which was a building constructed to honor the Aztec gods of rain and war. Templo Mayor was the center of religious activity in Tenochtitlán, and religion was very important to the Aztec people.

More than 140,000 people lived in Tenochtitlán at the height of the Aztec Empire, and it was the most populated city in Mesoamerica at the time. The island city was laid out in a grid pattern, and **aqueducts** were built to bring water to the city. Tenochtitlán was connected to the mainland by causeways, or raised roads over wetlands or water. Many artifacts have been recovered from the area that was once Tenochtitlán. It's now Mexico City, which is the capital of Mexico.

UNITED STATES

PACIFIC OCEAN

MEXICO

TENOCHTITLÁN

MESOAMERICA

Shown here is a model of what historians believe Templo Mayor looked like.

The ruins of Templo Mayor, shown here, have helped historians learn much about Aztec culture.

THE SOCIAL SYSTEM

Much of the Aztec civilization revolved around a **strict** system of social classes. Religion was central to Aztec culture, so priests were a respected class of Aztec people. Aztec nobles had many rights. They were typically well educated and allowed to wear fancy clothing and hold government positions. The rulers of the Aztec people were always members of the noble class.

This illustration shows a group of Aztec warriors. If a warrior was successful, he could move into a higher social class.

This image shows different Aztec social classes. It's easy to tell rulers from slaves based on the clothing they wore.

Another major class in this system was the common people. These people generally worked the land. As the Aztec civilization developed, more people became merchants and **artisans**, and they were another part of the class of common people.

Some Aztecs were slaves. People often became slaves as punishment for crimes. A slave's children weren't born into a life of slavery, and slaves could choose to purchase their freedom.

THE AZTEC LANGUAGE

The Aztec people spoke and wrote in a language called Nahuatl. This language is part of the Uto-Aztecan language family, which was made up of languages spoken in what's now western North America. The Nahuatl language is sometimes simply called Aztec. This language was originally written as pictures, and it was often found written on skins and paper and carved into stones.

People who study ancient languages are working to teach others the ancient Nahuatl language. This is a way for people of Aztec **descent** to connect with their history.

Words are formed in Nahuatl by combining prefixes (beginnings of words), suffixes (endings of words), and root words (main parts of words). This language also features repeating **syllables**, creating long words.

There are many forms of this language still in use. In fact, more than 1 million people in Mexico today still speak forms of Nahuatl.

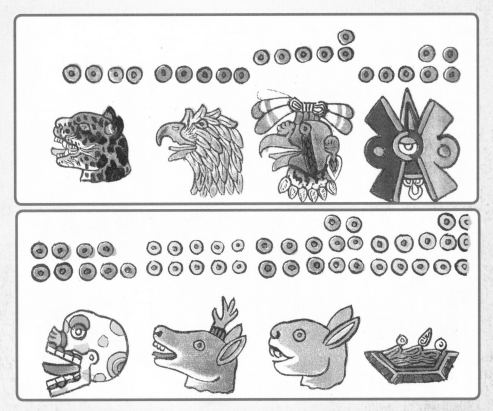

Shown here are pictures used by the Aztec people to represent, or stand for, important gods, animals, and elements in the Aztec calendar. Because the Aztec people didn't have an alphabet, they used pictures to express ideas.

BY THE NUMBERS

The Aztecs counted in sets of 20. A number system based on 20 is called a vigesimal system. To write numbers, the Aztecs used a series of dots. One dot represented the number one, and the numbers two, three, and four were represented by that number of dots. Five was written as five dots or a bar, and then dots and bars would be combined to make larger numbers. Ten was often written as a rhombus, or diamond. Twenty was a vase, shell, or flag. Similar to the Aztec alphabet, pictures were used to represent numbers, and every **power** of 20 was assigned a new picture or symbol.

This system could be a bit confusing. There could be multiple ways to make the same number, just as there are multiple ways to make change for a dollar bill using different coins.

Shown here is a page from an Aztec codex, or piece of ancient writing in book form. The dots used to represent numbers are clearly visible.

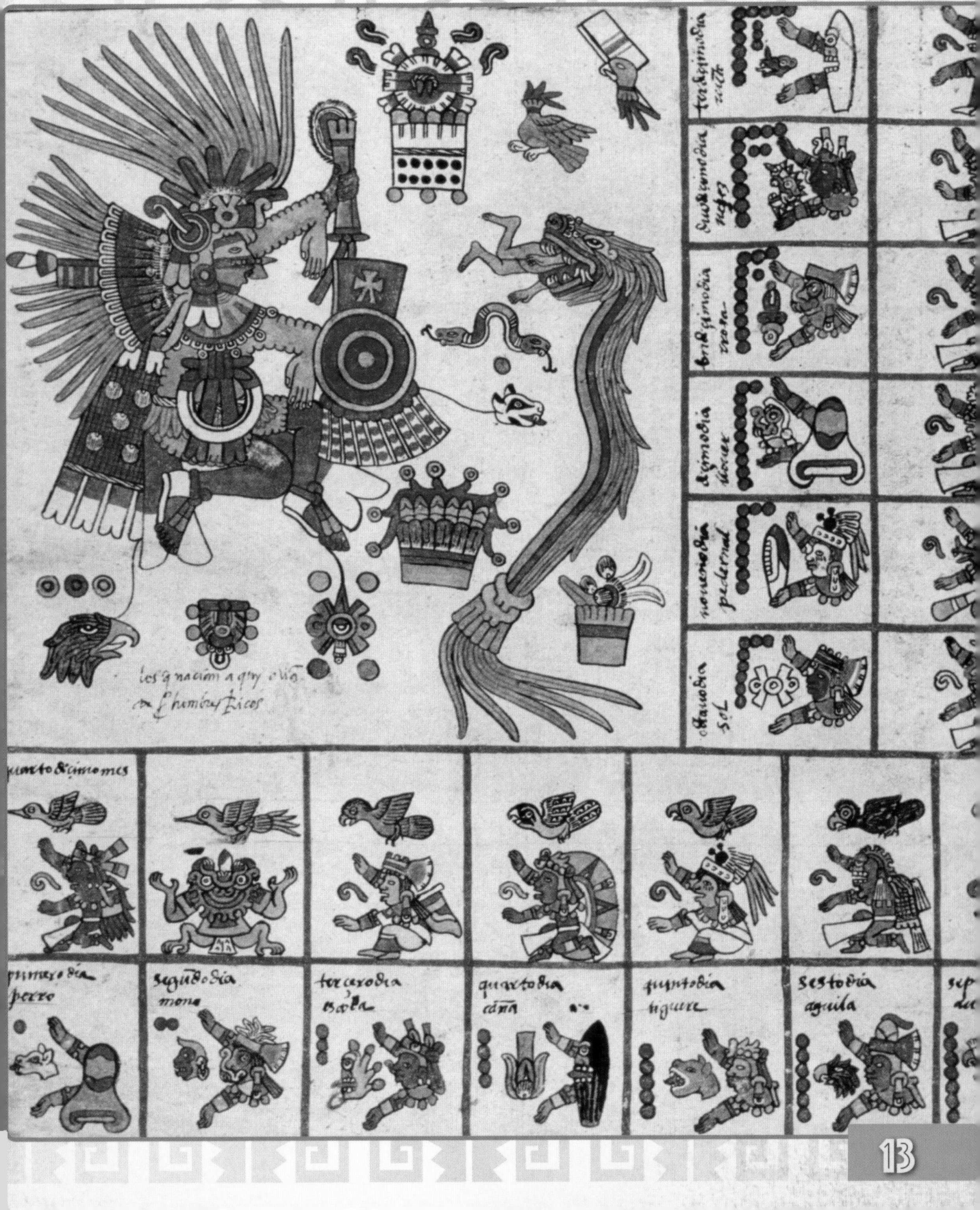

primero dia
perro
segudo dia
mono
quarto dia
caña
quinto dia
tigure
sesto dia
aguila

AZTEC RELIGION

Religion was central to Aztec culture. The Aztec people worshipped many gods. Because nature was very important in Aztec culture, many Aztec gods reflected some type of weather. One of the most important Aztec gods was the sun and war god, Huitzilopochtli.

Sacrifice was an important part of Aztec religion. The Aztecs were known for offering human sacrifices to their gods. Often, the people who were offered as human sacrifices were people who were conquered by the Aztecs. Human blood and human hearts were seen by many Aztecs as the most important offerings that could be made to their gods.

This image shows an Aztec priest offering a human sacrifice to Huitzilopochtli.

Quetzalcóatl was another important Aztec god. He was often shown as a feathered snake.

QUETZALCÓATL

HUITZILOPOCHTLI

Priests and priestesses were highly respected in Aztec society. Religious ceremonies were performed by a priest or priestess in a temple made specifically for that purpose. People can still visit the ruins of Aztec temples in Mexico today. The Aztecs also had an advanced calendar they used to keep track of religious ceremonies dedicated to their many gods.

FUNERALS AND THE AFTERLIFE

The Aztec people believed in an afterlife, and they thought how a person died helped determine where they went once they died. They believed that in order to reach the resting place for the dead, they had to go through trials in the nine levels of the underworld. This process was thought by the Aztecs to take four years, and people were buried with items that would help them complete the journey. These trials took place in Mictlan, or the underworld, which was ruled by Mictlantecuhtli, who was known as the god of the dead.

Aztec people wore masks, such as the one shown here, for different ceremonies. After a person died, a mask was placed on them to represent their spirit. This kind of mask is called a funerary mask.

Aztecs were generally cremated, or burned, after they died. This was especially true for nobles. They were wrapped while in a squatting position and then burned. In some special cases, bodies were buried instead. These bodies belonged to people the Aztecs believed didn't have to go through the trials of the underworld. These people included Aztecs who drowned or died from certain illnesses, as well as women who died in childbirth.

SUCCESSFUL FARMERS

The Aztec civilization was built on agriculture, or farming. The ability to farm successfully gave the Aztec people more time and resources to develop their advanced culture.

The Aztec people created gardens called chinampas for farming. Chinampas were manmade islands used to grow crops in lakes. The Aztecs used different farming **techniques**—including chinampas—to grow their most important crop: maize, or corn. They also grew beans, squash, tomatoes, and chilies. Sometimes, the Aztec people built terraces for farming. This involved creating flat areas on the sides of hills to make more usable land. Terraces allowed the Aztec people to farm in parts of the empire that had mountains and hills.

Farmers made up a large portion of the Aztec population. They were an essential part of Aztec society because agriculture was so important to the success of the Aztec Empire.

This illustration shows Aztec men making a chinampa. More chinampas can be seen in the background.

A CULTURE OF CITY-STATES

While farming allowed Aztec culture to flourish, a unified way of governing allowed their cultural identity to spread throughout the Aztec Empire. Although the Aztec Empire was made up of hundreds of city-states, which the Aztecs called *altepetl*, each city-state had the same basic government. A city-state was ruled by a leader called a *tlatoani*. The *tlatoani* of each city-state was a member of the noble class.

Eventually, three city-states grew to become the most powerful in the region: Texcoco, Tlacopan, and Tenochtitlán. They are known as the Triple Alliance. Tenochtitlán was the most important of these city-states, and it became the center of Aztec culture and the entire Aztec Empire. The ruler of Tenochtitlán was known as the *huey tlatoani*, which is a title close to what we'd call "emperor." If an emperor died, a new emperor was chosen by a council of nobles.

Shown here is what one of the entrances to the Aztec capital of Tenochtitlán was believed to have looked like.

ART, JEWELRY, AND CLOTHING

The Aztecs' art tended to focus on nature and the gods they worshipped. Many statues, masks, and other representations of the gods are found when archaeologists uncover the places where the Aztecs used to live. Ancient Aztec art was often lifelike, and many statues were quite detailed. Statues could be carved from wood or stone and varied in size from small to very large.

This Aztec two-headed serpent is made of turquoise and other stones.

This Aztec religious statue can be seen at the National Museum of Anthropology in Mexico City.

The Aztecs also used metals, including gold, in their artwork and jewelry. Aztec art also featured precious stones, such as turquoise, which is a blue or blue-green stone.

Aztec clothing was typically loose fitting and made of cotton or similar fibers, which helped keep them cool in the warm weather. The clothing people wore reflected their social class. Noble men often wore clothing and jewelry that was more decorative than what commoners or slaves wore. Nobles also wore cotton clothing, while common people wore clothing made of less comfortable fibers.

WARRIORS AND WEAPONS

The Aztecs were known as fierce warriors. They were very interested in expanding their empire and fought many battles in order to conquer more land. Successful warriors were treated with great respect in Aztec culture. They received special privileges.

All Aztec children had to go to school. There were different schools for young people who would become warriors and for members of the noble class. Aztec girls also went to school, but they weren't allowed to become warriors.

Warriors used weapons such as bows and arrows, clubs, spears, and lances. An Aztec warrior might also have used a special weapon called a *maquahuitl*. This weapon was like a wooden sword. It had sharp blades made of **obsidian** on both sides. Warriors used each of their weapons for a unique purpose, and they were taught how to use these weapons in school from the time they were teenagers.

Each Aztec warrior in this drawing is shown holding a *maquahuitl*.

Shown here is a statue of an Aztec warrior.

FUN AND GAMES

Although the Aztecs were fierce warriors, they also liked to have a good time. The Aztecs had many games and sports for all ages and social classes. Many games had some type of religious **significance**, and some games were even played as part of religious **rituals**. One game, which had many names, including *ullamaliztli* or tlachtli, was especially popular. The goal of the game was to get a ball through one of two stone hoops using the head, elbows, hips, and knees. This game was influenced by the Aztec people's connection to nature, as the court was meant to represent the heavens.

Aztec sports were often very violent. People sometimes died playing sports such as *ullamaliztli*, shown here.

Another popular game among the Aztecs was patolli. This was a game played on a cross-shaped board, and people would bet on the outcome of the game. Gambling was a big part of ancient Aztec culture. People placed bets during many games or sporting events.

This image from an Aztec codex shows Aztec people playing a game of patolli while an Aztec god watches them.

THE COLLAPSE OF A CULTURE

The Aztec culture was powerful, rich in religious history, and advanced beyond many other civilizations of its time. However, it fell after less than 300 years of existence. In 1519, Spanish explorer Hernán Cortés reached Aztec territory and was greeted with gifts and kindness from the Aztecs. He was there to conquer, but the relationship between the Aztecs and the Spanish began with diplomacy.

However, as Cortés and his men moved through Aztec land, he began to take charge and demand that the Aztecs view him as their ruler. The Spanish people also spread smallpox—a disease completely unfamiliar to the Aztecs— through the native population. Many Aztecs died as a result.

After many battles, Cortés officially conquered Tenochtitlán in 1521. The Aztec emperor, Montezuma II died before this while being held prisoner by the Spanish.

> While it seemed Cortés and his men initially came in peace, they eventually used their guns and horses to conquer the Aztec people.

WHAT WAS LEFT BEHIND

The ancient Aztecs had a very advanced culture, despite the fact that their great empire rose and fell within only a few hundred years. From sports to art and from architecture to weapons, the Aztecs had a reason for every part of their culture. Those reasons often revolved around pleasing their many gods.

Although many Aztec artifacts and belongings were lost when the Spanish conquistadors took over, the things that remain today teach us about the culture and society the Aztecs created. Some Aztec traditions have survived in modern times, and they're still practiced in Mexico.

Learning about Mesoamerican cultures, such as the ancient Aztec culture, is important. It gives us a better understanding of people that are different from us. It also helps us appreciate the advances made by ancient people who lived in the Western Hemisphere long before Europeans arrived.

GLOSSARY

aqueduct (AH-kwuh-duhkt): A channel constructed to move water from one place to another.

artisan (AAR-tuh-zuhn): A skilled worker who makes things with their hands.

conquistador (kahn-KEES-tuh-dor): A Spanish leader who conquered, or took over, people and land in the Americas during the 16th century.

custom (KUHS-tuhm): The usual way of doing things for a person or group.

descent (dih-SENT): The background of a person in terms of their family or nationality.

Mesoamerica (meh-zoh-uh-MEHR-ih-kuh): The southern part of North America and part of Central America that was—at one time—occupied by people with shared cultural features, such as the Maya and Aztecs.

obsidian (uhb-SIH-dee-uhn): A black, glassy rock formed by quickly cooling lava.

power (POW-uhr): The amount of times a number is repeated as a factor in a product of multiplication.

ritual (RIH-chuh-wuhl): An established form of a ceremony.

significance (sig-NIH-fuh-kuns): Importance or meaning.

strict (STRIHKT): Absolute, observed with great care.

syllable (SIH-luh-buhl): A unit of spoken language made up of one or more vowel sounds alone or combined with one or more consonant sounds before or after it.

technique (tehk-NEEK): A method of accomplishing a task.

unique (yoo-NEEK): Special or different from anything else.

INDEX

PRIMARY SOURCE LIST

Cover: Turquoise mosaic mask. Creator unknown. ca. 1400–1521. Cedro wood covered with turquoise, mother-of-pearl, conch shell, and cinnabar. Now kept at the British Museum, London, UK.

Page 7 (bottom): Skull sculpture at Templo Mayor. Creator unknown. ca. 1325–1521. Now part of the ruins of Templo Mayor visible in Mexico City, Mexico.

Page 16: Mask. Creator unknown. ca. 1400–1521. Wood. Now kept at the Walters Art Museum, Baltimore, MD.

Page 22: Double-headed serpent pectoral. Creator unknown. ca. 1400–1521. Cedro wood covered with turquoise, red thorny oyster shell, conch shell, and hematite. Now kept at the British Museum, London, UK.

WEBSITES

Due to the changing nature of Internet links, PowerKids Press has developed an online list of websites related to the subject of this book. This site is updated regularly. Please use this link to access the list: www.powerkidslinks.com/soac/azcul